What's a Zoo Do?

WHAT'S a ZOO Do?

JONATHAN WEBB

KPk
Key Porter Kids

Photographs: Brian Beck, 5, 8, 29 (above), 32, 36, 40, 44, 47, 48, 55, 76, 88; John Edwards, 26, 35, 58-59 (above), 66 (above), 66 (below), 67, 79; Francis X. Faigal/Metro Toronto Zoo, 37, 57 (below), 80 (below), 81 (above), 84; Frankfurt Zoo, 14, 29 (below); Friends of the Burnet Park Zoo, 6, 7; Stephen Homer, vi, 24, 49; Stephen Homer/First Light, 61 (above); London Zoological Society, 15 (above), 15 (below), 18, 19, 23; Franz Maier, 13, 17, 25, 53 (above), 64, 80 (above); Melbourne Zoo, 53 (below); Metro Toronto Zoo, 28, 41, 57 (above), 61 (below), 81 (below); New York Zoological Society, 39; Mark and Delia Owens, 72, 73; Lorraine Parow/First Light, 20; Philadelphia Zoological Society, 74; Taronga Zoo, 16; Ron Watts/First Light, ii; Jonathan Webb, 58 (left), 59 (right).

Canadian Catologuing in Publication Data

Webb, Jonathan, 1950–
    What's a zoo do?
    Includes index

ISBN 1-55013-609-7 (cloth)   1-55013-664-X (pbk.)

1. Zoos — Juvenile literature. 2. Zoo animals — Juvenile literature. I. Title.
QL76.W43 1995   J590'.74'4   C94-932506-6

Key Porter Books Limited
70 The Esplanade
Toronto, Ontario
Canada M5E 1R2

The publisher gratefully acknowledges the assistance of the Canada Council, the Ontario Arts Council, and the Ontario Publishing Centre.

PHOTOGRAPH ON PAGE 2: North American zoos have made a special effort to breed cheetahs, which are endangered in the wild.

Design: Annabelle Stanley
Electronic Layout: Jean Lightfoot Peters
Printed and bound in Hong Kong

95 96 97 98 99 6 5 4 3 2 1

For Nora, Harry, and Madeleine

CONTENTS

A GREAT BIG BABY

It was a hot summer night at the Burnet Park Zoo in Syracuse, New York. Chuck Doyle, the head elephant keeper, was the only person in the elephant barn. He was there to keep an eye on an elephant with a plugged nose.

At ten o'clock, Chuck noticed that things weren't right with another elephant. Romani bent her hind legs as if she wanted to sit down, but then straightened up again. She shifted her weight from one side to the other, as if disturbed or uncomfortable.

Chuck wondered if the time had finally come, the time everyone in the zoo had been waiting for, when Romani would give birth. He decided that she could be showing the early signs of labor — the muscle movements that would force the baby elephant out of its mother's body.

Chuck quickly telephoned the people he wanted to have in or near the barn if he was right: the two elephant keepers, the zoo

OPPOSITE PAGE: **When it's too cold for the elephants to swim in the pool outside, keepers hose them down indoors. They need to get wet regularly to have healthy skin.**

1

veterinarian and her assistant, the curator of mammals, and the zoo director. Some of them were in bed when he called. They were sleepy when they arrived at the barn. But the birth of an elephant is a rare and exciting event at a zoo. They wouldn't have missed this for anything.

At eleven o'clock, Carolee Wallace, the zoo veterinarian, announced that Romani was definitely in labor. At fifteen years of age, Romani was still young: elephants live almost as long as humans do. She had never had a baby before and had never seen another elephant give birth. Had she grown up in the wild, she would have spent time with other elephants of all ages. But, because she had lived most of her life in a zoo, with only a few elephants of about her own age, she didn't know anything about being a mother.

Chuck was concerned about the things Romani might not be able to do. A baby elephant is not likely to survive for long without the support and guidance of its mother. It needs her, especially, to give it milk. Sometimes elephants like Romani that have never spent time with young elephants refuse to have anything to do with their own. In one or two cases, first-time mothers have even tried to kill the baby. Chuck didn't want this to happen with Romani.

The zoo staff tried not to disturb Romani during her labor. Only Chuck and the two keepers she was used to went into her stall.

Now that she was hurting and unsure about what was happening, she looked to her keepers for comfort. She would lift a leg so they could pat it. Sometimes she made a sound like the bark of a sea lion, and Chuck would talk to her gently.

People at the zoo knew that Romani's labor could be for just a few hours, or as much as a day or more. It's the same with humans. Chances are, when your mother went into labor, no one knew exactly how long it would be before you were born. Chuck and the two keepers stayed with Romani while the others watched what was happening on a television monitor set up nearby. Three other elephants also watched from their places in the barn. Siri, Targa, and Shanthi munched hay and murmured to one another the way elephants do on a warm summer night. Chuck wanted them to see the birth, too. Then they, unlike Romani, would know something about having babies and being a mother. They would see the birth and learn from it.

The keepers stayed with Romani all night. The elephant continued to act as if she were uncomfortable. And she seemed to be confused and upset about what was happening to her.

At daybreak Romani was still in labor and apparently no closer to giving birth. Carolee examined the elephant again. She thought the baby might be in an awkward position in the birth canal, the passage in the mother's belly

3

WHAT'S A ZOO DO?

through which the baby travels when it is born. She thought it might even be stuck. She discussed the problem with other members of the zoo staff. They talked it over and decided to wait. But they were getting worried.

They knew that if the baby was stuck for too long, it would die, and that Romani might die, too.

By about six that morning, Chuck and all the others were nervous and upset. Carolee telephoned some of the veterinarians specializing in reproduction who taught at Cornell University in Ithaca, New York. Two of the university vets agreed to come and examine Romani. But it would take hours for them to get from their homes in Ithaca to the zoo in Syracuse and, to the people waiting at the zoo, it seemed like forever. All the zoo people could do was watch Romani and wait.

A New Day

At ten in the morning, the zoo opened its gates as usual. The other elephants were fed. Their stalls were cleaned. They were given water. They were hosed and scrubbed. It was business as usual everywhere except in Romani's stall. She swayed and bent her hind legs and stretched her trunk toward her keepers.

Finally, the specialists arrived. They talked to Carolee and Chuck. Then the keepers took their positions at each end of the elephant, one to maintain eye contact with the elephant and

The Large, Economy Size

The biggest elephant (more than 3.5 m/ 11 feet at the shoulders) ever kept in a zoo was an African elephant named Jumbo. He arrived in the London Zoo in 1865 from the Jardin des Plantes in Paris, and in 1882 he was sold to P.T. Barnum's circus in the United States.

4

LEFT: **A keeper at the National Zoological Park in Washington, D.C., cleans the rear foot of an Asian elephant. Elephants in zoos need a lot of care and are trained to allow their keepers to work closely with them.**

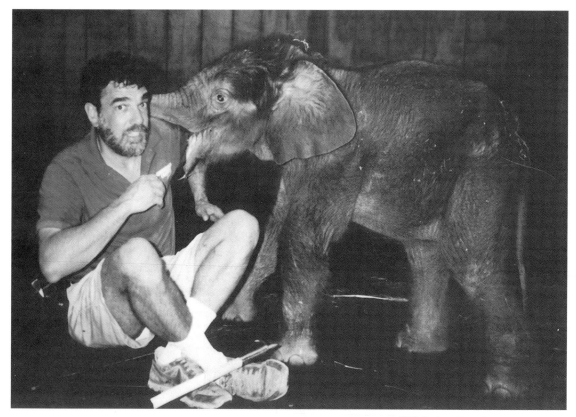

Chuck Doyle with Tundi just two days after the elephant's birth.

reassure her, the other to assist the visiting vets. One of the vets had hardly begun his examination when he called out, "Here it comes!"

Almost immediately, the feet appeared, and within minutes it was all over. A baby elephant lay on the floor.

Someone announced: "It's a girl!" Whoever it was spoke too soon — the baby elephant turned out to be a male. It weighed 102 kg (224 pounds) — about as much as the refrigerator in your kitchen at home. They called him Tundi.

Romani wasn't sure what had happened at first. She tried to help Tundi get to his feet. By the evening of his first day in the world, Tundi didn't need any help. He wobbled, then walked, then trotted around the barn.

In the next few days, Romani got used to having the calf underfoot. She let him take milk from her breast when he needed to, and he soon put on weight. Everyone breathed a sigh of relief to see that Romani was an ideal mother.

Tundi was already exploring the barn when he was just four days old.

7

GARDENS OF DELIGHT

Tundi was born, not in the Asian wilderness where his mother came from, but in a North American zoo. Because most of us today live in cities, we rarely get to see animals like Romani and Tundi in the wild. But things used to be different.

Two hundred years ago, North America was covered in forest, and so was a lot of Europe. Where there was forest, there were also wild animals. There were cougars in New England and grizzly bears in southern California. In parts of Europe packs of wolves were common and there was a species of buffalo called a wisent.

When settlers cut down the forests, made farms on the flat lands, and built cities in the valleys, they reduced the number of places where wild animals could live. Now cougars and grizzlies, wisents and wolves, and many other animals too, are gone from the places where they once were common.

By building cities and clearing land for farms,

OPPOSITE PAGE: The gorilla exhibit in Busch Gardens, Florida, has been made to look like an African rainforest.

9

and by making roads, railways, and airports to connect them, we changed the world we live in. And we may have lost something we really need: places that are beautiful and untouched by humans. Many people now try to make sanctuaries that are like small pockets of wilderness. In almost every city there are public parks, and in almost every backyard there is a garden. The ducks, geese, and swans that can be found in the parks, and the wild birds attracted to feeders in our gardens, remind us of the wilderness.

Zoos are often built in garden-like settings. Some new zoos are constructed on large parcels of land that look like wilderness. The animals in zoos are either species that might have lived in the area when it was a wilderness, or animals such as Romani, brought from countries far away. When you visit the zoo, you are, in a way, visiting the past. When you see cougars glide through the underbrush and wolves gather in a clearing, you are catching a glimpse of the world as it was before people changed it.

The Sun King's Garden

One of the first modern zoos was built in the middle of the seventeenth century at Versailles by King Louis XIV of France. Before it became a zoo, it was a garden. The king had cages placed among the neat paths, clipped hedges, and lush flowerbeds. If you had been able to visit it then, you might have been amazed to find yourself suddenly looking through bushes at the fierce face of a striped hyena or over roses at a young rhinoceros.

But, chances are, you would never have been invited to King Louis's garden. He was known as the Sun King because he was so rich and powerful that it seemed as if the world spun around him just as planets spin around the sun. The people who came to stay with him were mainly rich and powerful too.

Most people who lived in France in those days were poor. They had to pay taxes to the king but got very little in return. When Louis XIV died, his son became king, and his grandson after that. They continued to live in luxury while many ordinary people went hungry. By the time King Louis XVI came along, ordinary people were fed up. They took to the streets in what was later called the French Revolution. They killed the king and a lot of his friends and relatives and they threw many others in prison.

During the fighting, the zoo at Versailles was overrun by soldiers. Some of them were angry to see the king's antelopes and monkeys looking fat when the soldiers and their families often went hungry. They killed many of the animals for meat to feed their families. But when they came to some of the fiercer-looking animals, they decided that it might be better to be hungry soldiers than dinner for a hungry lion or bear. These animals survived the Revolution and were eventually given a new home, in 1794, at the Jardin des Plantes in Paris.

At Versailles, the zoo had been a sort of playground for a king who could have almost anything he wanted. But the Jardin des Plantes in Paris was different. It was run by scientists, and anyone could visit it. One of the scientists, Baron Georges Cuvier, later became famous for his animal studies. His work, and that of others who worked with him, gave zoos a new purpose. From about the beginning of the nineteenth century, people began to think of zoos not as private gardens but as public parks and scientific laboratories. Animals were captured and kept alive not just to amuse visitors but also so that scientists could study how they lived.

Modern Zoos

The London Zoological Society was formed in 1826, at a time when England was becoming the most powerful country in the world. English soldiers and sailors and the representatives of English companies traveled everywhere, from the Far East to Africa and North America. They brought back fruit and spices, lumber and furs, and sometimes live animals. Sailors were famous for the birds and monkeys they tried to tame and keep for company on their long voyages. Many of these animals ended up amid the jumble of other

A Gruesome Gift

The first animal at the London Zoo may have been a griffon vulture. It was the gift of a medical doctor, who kept it in the hospital where he taught anatomy, and where it ate the bits left over after classes came to an end. The vulture, named Dr. Brookes, after its original owner, lived at the zoo for 35 years. It died in 1861.

The zoo in Barcelona, Spain, has beautiful gardens for people to walk in.

goods that were unloaded from the sailing ships. Later they would be stored in the warehouses and sold in the shops that sprang up near the docks.

Many animals in the London Zoo were gifts from people who had traveled abroad. Others were bought from dealers who bought and sold animals around the docks. The collection of animals at the London Zoo quickly became one of the largest in the world because the port of London was the hub of a great empire.

Other European cities soon followed London's example and started zoos of their own. Amsterdam and Frankfurt, Berlin and

ABOVE: The journey from the wild to the zoo was difficult and frightening for the animals. A crane was used to lift them out of the ship's hold and onto the dock.

Budapest, Manchester and Munich, all built zoos in the middle decades of the nineteenth century. The first zoo in North America opened in Philadelphia in 1874. It was followed by many others, including New York (the Bronx Zoo), Chicago, and later San Diego. Like the first modern zoos in Paris and London, these were designed to be both gardens and laboratories. Zoos have changed a lot over the last two hundred years, but the chief reasons for their existence — to entertain the public and provide facilities for scientists — remain the same. Only one significant new purpose has

ABOVE: **Ladies and gentlemen stroll on the lawn in front of the Monkey House at England's London Zoo in 1835.**

LEFT: **Women and children tour the Monkey House at the London Zoo, about 1905.**

been added, now that wilderness has nearly disappeared, and that is to help conserve the animals that remain.

What Zoos Do

The first zoos were built to amuse and amaze us. They were small so that visitors didn't have

FAVORITE ZOO ANIMALS

A zoo director once complained about the public who came to the zoo. "That rhinoceros over there cost $12 000," he said, "and there are just six people in front of the cage. Everybody else crowds in front of a $45 collection of monkeys."

The zoo animals the public likes best are not always those that are most rare or expensive. Many people like pandas and koalas, which are rare — very rare in the case of the panda. But other animals, including apes, monkeys, big cats, and wolves are also popular. What attracts people to particular kinds of animals?

Koalas are always among the favorite zoo animals.

People like best the animals whose faces are most similar to human faces. Looked at from the front, all the animals just mentioned have eyes, nose, and mouth in about the same positions. It's easy to look at their faces and imagine

to walk very far. The cages were bare boxes made of iron bars in which the animals were completely exposed: they had no privacy, no place to hide. Often the animals were frightened and poorly fed. Many died at a young age. It would not be true to say that the animals were always badly treated. There were

you know what the animals are thinking or feeling. Because they look a bit like people, we think of them as having human expressions and personalities.

Some people think pandas are cute, even though they can be bad-tempered and dangerous. Other people, ignoring the razorlike claws, believe koalas are cuddly. Yet others persist in thinking that lions are just oversized cats and that wolves are big, affectionate dogs.

Even when the keepers who know them best agree that some animals, such as great apes, are typically gentle and patient, they emphasize that they are all still unpredictable and wild.

The monkeys that the director complained about may not be as much like people as we sometimes think they are, but they will probably continue to attract bigger crowds than the rhinoceros, which doesn't look like a human at all.

Snowflake, the unusual white gorilla at the zoo in Barcelona, has become known to zoo visitors all over Europe.

No Visitors!

The National Zoo's Conservation and Research Center in Virginia and the St. Catherines Wildlife Conservation Center in Georgia (operated by the New York Zoological Society) are closed to the public. Rare species, such as the scimitar-horned oryx, Père David's deer, ring-tailed lemur, and Burchell's zebra, are raised in these parks.

The Camel House at the London Zoo in the 1830s.

18

people then who understood what animals needed, just as there are today. But in general, zoos in those days were designed with the visitors, not the animals, in mind.

Today, we know a lot more about animals than people did then. Modern zoos still exist partly to delight the millions of visitors who wander down their tree-lined paths on summer afternoons. But they also exist to give satisfactory homes to animals. This takes knowledge and experience on the part of the people who work in the zoo. In the following pages, you will see how zoo directors, architects, builders, scientists, veterinarians, and keepers work together to provide safe, secure, and natural-looking homes for the hundreds of species of animals that live within their walls.

The Asian elephant that gave rides at the London Zoo in 1905 was called Dr. Jim.

19

ANIMAL CITIES

Cities are a habitat made for people rather than animals. Of course, people are animals, but we often think of ourselves as different.

You could think of a zoo as a special kind of city that provides habitats for many different kinds of animals. The paths in the zoo, like streets in a city, take you from one exhibit to another. And the exhibits, like buildings in a city, contain the things animals need.

People who run zoos have to know all about the needs of the animals in their care. They have to know what they eat, of course, but that's just a start. They also have to know when they sleep — many animals sleep during the day rather than the night. And they have to know where they sleep. Some animals, such as bats, hang from the roofs of caves, while others, such as badgers, dig nests in the ground. They have to know whether the animals need water to roll around in as well as to drink. Elephants, for example, often cover themselves with mud:

OPPOSITE PAGE: **This male lion can either take refuge in its den or wander into its yard.**

21

it helps to cool them off and keep their skin healthy. And wild hippopotamuses usually spend most of the day in water and come out only when the sun goes down. The zoo has to make a habitat for each animal in which it can do the things that come naturally.

Cage, Yard, and Holding Area

Not so long ago, zoos often did a poor job of giving animals the things they needed. Bears were almost always kept in pits, for example, which wasn't anything like what they were used to in the wild. This method of containing bears sometimes led to unexpected problems, too, like the time there was so much rain at the zoo in Paris that the pits were flooded and the bears had to cling to their climbing posts to escape the water.

The exhibits where other animals were kept were usually just empty cages. These cages were put inside buildings that housed similar animals. All apes and monkey-like creatures were in the monkey house; all members of the cat family were in the lion house; and all snakes and lizards were in the reptile house. These buildings were made to be comfortable for the people who came to look at the animals, not for the animals themselves.

If you could have visited one of these zoos, you would have been able to see the animals at all times because they had nowhere to hide. The keepers fed and cleaned up after them right

The bear pit at the London Zoo in 1835. The man in the top hat is offering the bear a bun on the end of a stick.

there in front of you. The animals themselves ate and slept and played — and got sick and had their young — all inside the same cage.

In these conditions, only the smallest animals could get the exercise they needed. Small mammals, such as jerboas and shrews, might be reasonably comfortable spending all day in a cage, but any larger animal was bound to suffer. So the people who designed zoos began to add a yard to the cage. The cage remained inside a building, but now each cage was connected by a gate to an outdoor enclosure.

In both the simple cage and the improved cage-and-yard systems, all animals were treated pretty much alike. It didn't make any difference that wild lions, for example, are most at home in dry, open country while tigers thrive in moist forests. Nor did it matter that orangutans in the wild find food and make their nests in the tops of trees while gorillas usually sleep and forage on or near the forest floor. There was rarely anything in the yard that was like the animal's natural environment.

When architects and curators began to consider how different the animals were from one another, instead of how similar, they began to make zoo enclosures more interesting and complicated. The most obvious change was that the viewing areas, where the animals usually spend the day, were made to look more natural.

You are no longer likely to see tigers and lions, or gorillas and orangutans, in cages next to one another. Now you might see lions in an exhibit that looks like an African savannah, and tigers in a setting like an Asian forest. Zoos often show gorillas in enclosures that have room for them to wander on the ground and provide orangutans with ropes and poles to climb and shelves to sit on.

As a rule, zoos now group animals from the same part of the world near each other. One part of the zoo may be made to look like the forests of southeast Asia, another like central

Africa, and so on. This arrangement (sometimes called zoogeographic) makes it easier for visitors to understand how the animals have adapted to their natural habitat. The tiger's black stripes look like dark shadows, making it seem almost to disappear against a sun-splattered background. In the same way, the lion's dust-colored coat blends into a field of dry grass. The great apes, too, look more comfortable when their homes are suited to

ABOVE: Good zoo exhibits show visitors what the animals' wild habitat is like. This wolf is obviously at home in its wooded enclosure.

OPPOSITE PAGE: Orangutans are immensely strong, so the swings and toys in their exhibit have to be built extra tough.

Is it real?

The rocks in the baboon enclosure look real, but they're not. They are not even solid. Underneath what looks like rock is a structure made of steel tubing covered by a skin of steel mesh. On top of the mesh, a kind of cement is shaped and molded to look like rock. When it dries, it's hard and smooth and can be cleaned easily. Behind the "rock" there may be keepers' rooms, cages, and holding pens for the animals.

The people who design and build zoos have to create enclosures that are attractive to visitors, easy for the keepers to clean, and suitable for the animals. The enclosures also have to be safe, to keep animals in and visitors out. It would be surprising if a site could be found that met all these conditions naturally. Usually, the architect and builders have to fake at least some of it.

Why does the lion often lounge on the rock at the front of its enclosure? A visitor might think it's merely basking in the sun. Yet the lion lounges on the same rock on cool, cloudy days. The answer is built right into the "rock," where an electric heater has been installed. The lion is attracted to the warmth of the heater, and the public is attracted to the easy-to-see lion.

The trees in the gorilla enclosure are real. But gorillas have a habit of picking at things and would soon destroy the bark of real trees. To protect the trees, the trunks are wrapped in a fiberglass skin. It looks like bark but is harder, and the gorillas mostly leave it alone.

Of course, not everything at the zoo is manufactured. The sand and the grass and the mud are real. And so are the animals.

Carl Hagenbeck's zoo in Stellingen, near Hamburg, Germany, was the first in the world to make natural-seeming exhibits using concrete to look like rock.

their needs. The orangutan uses its enormous strength to haul itself up a long rope as if it were climbing a jungle vine. And the gorilla clasps its arms around its shoulders and ducks its head when a shower bursts upon it just as it would in a downpour in equatorial Africa.

In addition to making more natural-looking exhibits, zoo designers have made another significant change to the layout of the modern zoo. Behind the exhibits, they have constructed buildings, yards, and holding areas that visitors rarely see. Unlike the public buildings, these don't have to suit human visitors, but can be designed purely for the animals. The holding pen may provide a safe and quiet place for an animal that has just arrived at the zoo and is not yet settled into its new home. It may provide privacy for animals that are mating, or for a female animal that is about to give birth. There may also be stalls or cages where keepers can examine animals at close quarters, and where veterinarians can treat those that are sick. Some of the most important zoo work is done in these areas hidden from public view.

Invisible Boundaries

Many animals are territorial. They live in the wild within well-defined areas that they defend against others of their kind. Wolf packs and groups of chimpanzees, for example, chase away strangers of their own species that come too close to their home ground. Male bears of

---

Born to Be Wild

What's the most difficult animal to keep alive in a zoo? In fact many species just don't do well in zoos. Usually it's because zookeepers don't know enough about an animal's diet or because they can't supply the food that it needs. Among the most difficult are duck-billed platypuses, panda bears, and proboscis monkeys.

A kookaburra in a large holding enclosure. Sunlight floods in through the overhead skylight.

all species (with the possible exception of polar bears) drive other male bears out of the territory they regard as their own. And the males of some species, including fur seals, become territorial during the breeding season, when they compete with one another to mate with females.

Instead of staking out a territory of a certain size and shape, as they would in the wild, animals in a zoo are given a territory by their keepers. Most animals eventually come to accept these artificial boundaries. Time and consideration may be needed, however, to help an animal adjust.

ABOVE: When the penguin pool was built in the London Zoo in England in the 1930s, people thought it was wonderful. Unfortunately, it was an awful place to keep penguins. There are no penguins in it now.

LEFT: The Frankfurt Zoo in Germany was among the first in the world to put a real iceberg inside a building where penguins could live as if they were home in Antarctica.

They have to adjust to the constant presence of people, among other things. Many animals instinctively regard humans as their enemy. Scientists have found that a wild animal takes little notice of a person who is far away, but it gets nervous if a person walks toward it. At a certain point, the animal either threatens the intruder or runs away. If you have ever tried to get close to a chipmunk or squirrel, for example, you probably saw it scamper away when you were within 3 to 3.5 m (3 to 4 yards) of it. Scientists call this distance — the distance at which an animal runs away or takes flight — the flight distance. The flight distance varies from one species to another.

A howler monkey in the wild, for example, may let a person approach to within 18 to 27.5 m (20 to 30 yards) before it takes to the trees. An ostrich may turn tail when someone is within 137 m (150 yards). And an American bison may flee when people are within 228 m (250 yards).

Zoos almost always put animals in enclosures that are smaller than their flight distance in the wild. This means that a howler monkey in a cage smaller than 27.5 m (30 yards) across is going to be scared right away. The people around it are too close for comfort. The same is true of an ostrich in an enclosure smaller across than 137 m (150 yards) or an American bison in one smaller than 228 m (250 yards). The danger is that an animal fresh from the wild will become

Now That's a Crowd!

More than six million people visit the Ueno Zoo in Tokyo, Japan, every year, making it the most popular zoo in the world.

frightened in a small enclosure and try to escape.

Several years ago at one large American zoo, a recently captured zebra arrived from Africa. It was pushed out of the crate in which it had traveled into a small, fenced enclosure. It panicked, galloped into the fence, broke its neck, and died.

The dealer who sold the zebra to the zoo had recommended that the keepers open one end of the crate and let the animal stay inside until it made up its own mind to come out. The crate, for the zebra, had become a home and hiding place. If the dealer's advice had been followed, the animal might have come to accept its new home.

Zookeepers have learned from accidents like this, and most are careful now when they introduce new animals to the zoo. They know that if an animal has a sheltered, familiar place within the zoo enclosure, its flight distance usually becomes shorter. It gets used to the presence of people outside its enclosure because it becomes accustomed to being left mostly alone inside. The same may be true of a chipmunk or squirrel in the wild. If it gets used to your presence near its nest, and you haven't chased it or made threatening moves, it may let you get quite close.

Most animals in the zoo are given a box or den to hide and sleep in. When they have got used to it, they usually gain the confidence to explore outside. Their flight distance

By the Numbers

The biggest animal collections in the world (not counting fish and invertebrates) are the London Zoological Society (approximately 6000 individual animals); Berlin Zoo (approximately 5000 individuals); Bronx Zoo (approximately 4300 individuals); and San Diego Zoo (approximately 3900 individuals).

gradually becomes shorter and they become at least partly tame.

Zoo animals have to tolerate not only visitors but also keepers. Hoofed animals such as elephants, deer, antelopes, and zebras may come to regard the keeper as part of the herd. They pay little attention when he or she brings in the hay or starts to shovel away the dung.

In some zoos, the keepers never enter an enclosure that contains large or dangerous animals such as bears, big cats, or great apes.

WHAT DO ZOO ANIMALS EAT?

In most zoos, the food is brought into a central kitchen supply depot, or commissary, where it is sorted out and distributed to the different departments. The list of foods that come into the commissary is astonishing.

A zoo's commissary staff prepares a variety of fresh and packaged foods for the animals each day.

Instead, they move the animals into a separate enclosure, or "shift" cage, while the main enclosure is being cleaned. Most animals move willingly from one enclosure to another if they know there is a food reward. Their keepers make the moves a part of the daily routine. They may put a bear's morning meal in the outdoor enclosure and its evening snack inside, so in the morning the bear goes willingly outside, and in the evening waits for the chance to get back inside.

Some items you would expect, such as fresh vegetables, hay, grain, fish, and cuts of meat. But what about crickets, baby mice, and Monkey Chow?

All kinds of birds, small mammals, and amphibians eat insects. It would be hard to supply them with the variety and quantity of tiny insects they would capture for themselves in their natural environment. Crickets, however, contain many of the nutrients these animals need, and they can be raised on farms especially to feed zoo animals. A large zoo may bring in hundreds of thousands of crickets each year.

The mice are chiefly for the snakes. (Birds of prey — falcons and hawks, for example — may also eat them.) Many snakes eat only living prey in the wild, but in most zoos, the mice are already dead. The keepers have to learn a trick of wiggling and twisting the mice when they offer them to the snakes so the snakes will think they're alive and strike at them.

It is almost impossible to provide some animals with their natural diet. Wild chimpanzees, for example, might range widely through a tropical forest, dining on fruit, nuts, berries, various kinds of vegetation, and even a few small animals. A considerate zookeeper tries to offer the chimps a modest variety of similar food, but he will supplement it with a packaged food — one is called Monkey Chow — that combines the essential ingredients for a balanced and healthy diet.

The Great Escape

In the summer of 1979 a pair of Japanese macaques, or snow monkeys, in Ohio's Columbus Zoo swam across the moat around their "monkey island," climbed up a hose that had been carelessly left hanging over the wall, and hit the road. Over the next six months they traveled more than 160 km (100 miles), eventually reaching the outskirts of Cleveland, Ohio, before they were finally captured.

Walls, Fences, and Moats

A group of gorillas in an English zoo once found the gate to their quarters ajar on Christmas Day. They set off down the road. It was late afternoon: most of the people in the neighborhood must have been sitting down to supper. In any case, the gorillas met no one. When they came to a house with an open door, they sauntered in and surprised the family at the dining-room table. The gorillas, being sociable animals, entered into the spirit of the occasion and helped themselves. A member of the family made a frantic call to the zoo and keepers came running. The gorillas were easily persuaded to return to their enclosure, but they took dinner with them.

Most animals tend to remain inside their enclosures once they are used to them. Some won't even leave when a gate is left open by accident. Others escape when they get the chance but come back on their own after they have explored the world outside. Some zoo people say that if they have done their job properly and given the animals what they need, then the animals won't try to escape. When an animal does try to get out, it may only be to find a quiet place, for example, or shelter from the hot sun. If the enclosure is fixed to provide peace and shade, they won't be inclined to wander.

Nevertheless, some animals are naturally talented escapers. Elephants have been known

to use the tips of their trunks to turn on water taps when they're thirsty. (One keeper said that he wouldn't mind except that they never bothered to shut the water off after they had satisfied their thirst.) With the same dexterity, elephants can lift latches and turn handles to open doors. Moose have muscular snouts with which they, too, can open gates that aren't locked. (No other members of the deer family have this ability.) And all apes are smart and have nimble fingers and will escape from quarters that aren't locked up tight.

Other animals escape by digging, climbing, jumping, or squeezing through tiny openings. Badgers and hedgehogs are especially clever at slipping through gaps in, or under, fences. Sloth

People almost never saw gorillas in zoos before the 1950s. Alfred, in England's Bristol Zoo, was among the first.

A water moat keeps gibbons and visitors apart at the Miami MetroZoo in Florida.

bears have the ability to shinny up smooth, vertical bars. And an adult polar bear once leapt from a water-filled moat to clamber over the top of a 3-m (8-foot)-high wall.

In the first zoos, escapes were prevented by either keeping the animals in pits or building high, barred walls around them. Pits are rarely used now because it seems cruel to keep an animal in a hole in the ground. Bars are still used, but they block the view and make the

36

zoo seem like a prison. Designers working with keepers have invented better ways to contain animals.

Perhaps the most popular way is to dig a dry or water-filled moat all around the enclosure. Most apes are wary of water, and a river or moat usually stops them in their tracks. If water is put around animals that can't swim, however, it is important to make it not too deep. Gorillas have sometimes fallen into a moat by accident and drowned.

Another problem with water barriers is that occasionally an animal that is supposed to be afraid of water will jump in anyway. At Chester Zoo in England, for example, soon after they

The water is extra cold in the polar bears' pool at the Metro Toronto Zoo in Canada. Visitors can see what great swimmers the bears are by looking through windows in the walls of the pool.

had put a moat around the ape exhibit, staff found a chimpanzee wading across to the other side. Nobody had told her she wasn't supposed to do that! The staff solved the problem by installing an electrified wire along the water's edge. Electrified, or "hot," wires are now commonly used around other exhibits, too.

Dry moats are often used to contain large mammals. Usually they are constructed with a steep slope on the animal's side and a high vertical wall on the visitor's side. If an animal falls or is pushed into the moat, it won't usually be hurt: the slope lets it slide rather than fall straight down. Often steps are cut into the slope so the animal can climb back out.

In some zoos, plants and mounds of earth are used with moats to create surprising visual effects. The exhibit may be on a plateau slightly higher than the platform where visitors gather. Between the exhibit and the platform there might be a mass of bushes and trees. Visitors looking past the leaves may get the feeling there is nothing between them and the animals. The animals may seem so close that visitors may even wonder, for a moment, if they're safe. They can't see the deep trench that lies between the animals and them.

The Bronx Zoo in New York has an exhibit that has been widely imitated. The African waterhole exhibit, where waterbucks and antelopes are displayed, is just behind a big rocky shelf where lions bask in the sun. It appears to visitors that the lions, waterbucks, and antelopes — predators and their prey — are all together on the same piece of land. But, of course, the exhibits are separated by a deep moat, and the waterbucks and antelopes are in no danger of becoming dinner for the pride of lions.

Fences Are for People

In a modern zoo, exhibits for large animals often look simply like open pieces of land. The

The African waterhole exhibit at the Bronx Zoo.

Peacocks are often allowed to wander anywhere within the walls of a zoo. They are too quick for visitors to get close to them, and as long as they get everything they need in the zoo, they tend not to run away.

land may be enclosed by a wall or moat. Somewhere behind this viewing area, out of sight, there may be a building and a holding area. Exhibits like this make up a large part of the zoo.

Smaller animals adapt to smaller enclosures. But even when the exhibits are small and situated indoors, there may also be a separate viewing area, den, and holding pen. Zoo-keepers try to tend to the different needs of the small as well as the large animals in their care.

Birds, of course, present different challenges

for zookeepers. A moat won't stop an animal that can fly over it. However, a few species of birds tend to stay close to home even when there is no barrier between them and the outside world. Peacocks, for example, are often given the run of the zoo. They strut on the lawns and utter their startling screeches from the tops of low walls. When it's time for supper, they return to their keepers. Swans, geese, and ducks may nest in tall grass near fresh water as long as they are not disturbed by visitors. Other

Lions gather in the den provided for them at the Metro Toronto Zoo. In the past, lions lived in mountainous regions as well as the plains of Africa. They are well adapted to survive cold weather.

birds, such as cranes, are prevented from flying by having their wings clipped.

Many species of birds are kept in large, light, and airy buildings, where there is ample space for them to establish their individual territory and stretch their wings. Often these buildings, filled with tropical trees, flowers, and bushes,

UNWANTED VISITORS

Zoos offer such comfortable quarters for their inhabitants that other animals are always trying to break in to share the easy life. Pigeons, skunks, cats, rats, mice, and squirrels are among the many animals that zoos have to watch out for. They eat the food meant for the zoo animals. They may damage the exhibits. And most dangerous of all, they may spread diseases that could lead to disaster.

Of course, the intruders may find themselves taking on more than they bargained for. Gorillas have caught small birds in their quick hands. And while elephants eat mainly grass, leaves, and bits of trees, and are supposed to be afraid of mice, one keeper swears he has seen an elephant calmly step on a mouse, sweep it up in its agile trunk, and swallow it.

are especially beautiful. Visitors walking through them may find no barriers obstructing their view. When they do come up against a fence or wall, chances are it is meant mainly to keep people away from birds' nests and exotic greenery.

Keeping animals inside their enclosures is not the zookeepers' toughest job. The real problem is often to keep people out of the enclosures and away from the animals. It's so tough sometimes that keepers get fed up and joke that the public should not be allowed into the zoo at all.

Only a few people cause all the trouble. Some individuals, for example, refuse to believe that wild animals can be dangerous. They try to pet the lions or tease the bears. Occasionally, a visitor is badly mauled or even killed. Vandals sometimes attempt to torture or kill the animals, and criminals have been known to steal birds, reptiles, or monkeys, so they can sell them to collectors.

Zoos have to be ready for the worst. But they have to be ready for regular people, too, like the loud and lively crowds that come to visit on holiday weekends. There are wide paths for visitors to walk on; miniature trains to ride; restaurants and souvenir and gift shops to visit; and places to sit and rest your feet. Well-planned zoos have plenty of washrooms — including one wherever there's a stream or waterfall. Some of the zoo staff — the guides, security guards, cleaning staff, and ticket takers, for example — are there mainly to look after visitors. Many others, however, work with the animals in the other, mostly hidden part of the zoo. You could call them zoo people.

43

ZOO PEOPLE

Zoo people are special. Animals are the most important thing in their life. Some zoo people are happier with the animals they work with than they are with other people.

Many zoo people lived with animals when they were children. One man who now runs a big American zoo admitted that when he was a boy, he kept turkey vultures in the garage and snakes in a box under his bed. (He didn't tell his parents about the snakes.) He says now that he is sorry he kept wild animals like that, trapped in boxes and small cages, unable to live naturally. He didn't know any better when he was young, but he learned a great deal about animals by looking after them.

A lot of zoo people have pets at home. They keep everything from dogs and cats to birds, snakes, and lizards. There are keepers who train wild horses in their spare time. One man, after years of working in a zoo, learned to train llamas. He quit his job at the zoo and now

OPPOSITE PAGE: **A keeper shows off a boa constrictor. Most zoos encourage visitors to talk to keepers and allow them to see some of the animals at close range.**

45

takes people on camping trips in the mountains of California. He uses llamas to carry their gear.

Because they are interested in animals, zoo people have a way of stumbling upon unusual animals to take care of. In Toronto a few years ago, two black caimans (a species of small alligator) were taken away from some criminals who had tried to smuggle them into Canada. The customs officers asked the staff at the Metro Toronto Zoo to help. A staff member offered to look after the caimans until a home could be found for them. He kept them in the basement of his house. The caimans seemed to be okay there, but for some reason they made the other people in the house nervous. Perhaps it was the sight of their rows of gleaming white teeth.

The Keepers

The people who work most closely with the animals in the zoo are the keepers. Their job is to take care of the animals. They feed them and clean up after them. In the morning, they move the animals from their sleeping quarters to the exhibits. At night, they put them back.

It is also the keeper's job to make sure the animals are healthy. Because keepers spend more time with the animals than anyone else, they know best the personality and habits of each one. The keepers are the first to notice when an animal that normally eats well is no longer hungry. They notice when an animal that is normally frisky becomes slow-moving or

> ### Danger!
> Zookeepers get hurt when they forget that any wild animal can be dangerous. A male deer in rutting season can be as dangerous as a leopard or a puff adder. But more keepers are hurt by elephants than anything else. It's easy to remember that vipers, for example, can be deadly, but elephants are so intelligent and seem so friendly that their keepers sometimes forget to be careful.

46

sleepy. They notice when an animal's fur is less glossy than usual or when its eyes are dull.

Every day, the keepers make notes about the animals they take care of on a computer or in a book called a log. Often when something is wrong, they fix it themselves. If an animal has cut itself on a broken section of fence, they may clean the wound and treat it with an antiseptic ointment. (They would also fix the fence, or make sure that someone else did.) If one animal is not getting its fair share of food because other animals push it aside at feeding time, the keeper may feed it separately.

When something goes wrong that isn't easily fixed, the keeper may talk to a supervisor about it. Other people may be brought in to help. The notes the keeper makes in the log are useful when problems crop up. Other keepers can read them to find out what has changed in an animal's behavior or daily routine. Often these small changes give clues pointing to a bigger problem.

This black caiman was taken away from smugglers by customs officers. It eventually found a home in the Metro Toronto Zoo.

Love and a Long Life

Some keepers talk about the animals they look after just as if they were people. They may say that an elephant is a "bad-tempered so-and-so," that a chimpanzee is a "fussy creature," or a tiger is an "old darling." Keepers often have their favorites. They soon learn which animals are full of mischief and which need to be left alone. The best keepers remember these quirks and treat the animals according to their individual needs.

For much of the nineteenth century, exotic animals were more likely to be seen in menageries and circuses than in zoos. People didn't get around as much in those days as they do now, so fewer people were able to see the big zoos. The menageries and circuses took wild animals on the road! They traveled from town fairgrounds to village greens all over Europe and North America. Menageries were just animal shows, while circuses also had clowns, jugglers, and acrobats. Circus animals, unlike the animals

A keeper at the Baltimore Zoo in Maryland has his notebook handy to record the behavior of the black-footed penguins that are gathered around him.

48

in menageries, were often trained to do tricks.

In both menageries and circuses, the animals were moved from place to place in cages built onto wagons, which were pulled by teams of horses. (Later they traveled in trucks and trains.) The roads were rough in those days. Even people in carriages found traveling uncomfortable.

The animals were also poorly fed. People often had no idea what food an animal from a faraway place was used to eating. Elephants, which should be given hay and leaves and tree branches, were fed bread and beer. Apes, which need fruit and berries, sometimes got nothing but meat. Even though the keepers did things we now know are wrong, however, the animals often lived a long time. Many

When animals, like these Bactrian camels, are newly arrived from other countries, they must spend time in separate pens while vets make sure they're healthy. The keepers' masks protect the animals from any diseases the keepers may be carrying.

49

mated and had babies.

Zoo animals today generally are more comfortable than those animals were. They have bigger, cleaner cages and better food. And they don't have to put up with the almost constant traveling. Why, then, did animals in circuses and menageries often live longer than zoo animals? Many people think it's because they were looked after by keepers who spent their lives with them.

In the old menageries and circuses, animals and keepers were constantly together. They worked, ate, washed, and cleaned up together. Sometimes they slept in the same cage or wagon. They rarely were out of one another's sight. The animals were loved and understood, and that, probably, was more important to them than the food, cage, and bumpy ride.

Some zookeepers today are almost as close to the animals as the old circus hands were. A few have worked at the same zoo with the same animals for twenty or thirty years or even longer. There is no question about why they decided to work at a zoo: they wanted to spend their lives taking care of animals. The animals they look after are lucky. They live longer, happier lives than animals in zoos where a new keeper replaces another one every couple of years.

Zoo Work

Not everyone who works in a zoo is a keeper. A zoo, like a city, is a complicated place. There

---

Everyone's Idea of a Good Time

Zoos are probably the single most popular form of entertainment in the world. More people visit zoos than go to football or baseball games, or attend theaters, cinemas, or concerts.

are lots of different jobs to be done.

A city has a works department to look after roads, water, and buildings; shops to supply food; police to enforce the law. It has buses and trains to move people and hospitals to tend the sick.

A zoo works in much the same way. There are people who make sure the paths are level, the water supply adequate, and the buildings clean. There are people who buy and prepare food. Security staff, like police officers, maintain order. Often there are buses and trains to take people around the exhibits and people who drive and look after them. And there is usually a clinic where veterinarians do their best to make sick animals well again.

The person in charge of the zoo is called the director. Some directors started out as keepers. Some are scientists or veterinarians. At least one director worked as a city manager before taking the job at the zoo.

Like city mayors, directors have to make sure that all the people who work for the zoo, from the ticket collectors at the front gate to the people who take out the garbage, are doing their jobs. They have to make sure that the news about the zoo's good work is made known to people who live in the vicinity. And they may have to raise money for the zoo, by persuading individuals and corporations to help pay for new buildings or animals. Directors aren't able to spend a lot of time with the animals. A few, however, sometimes take a break from their other tasks to walk around the zoo. Then they can see for themselves that the exhibits are tidy, the animals fit, and the staff working hard to take care of them.

After the director, the people next in charge of the animals are the curators. There may be a curator for each kind of animal. There could be, for example, a curator of mammals, a curator of birds, and a curator of reptiles and amphibians. Some curators used to be keepers. Others are scientists with university degrees in biology or zoology. It's important to love and respect animals if you want to work in a zoo, but it's also important to know how they live. This is why many keepers these days are scientists, too.

Curators make sure the animals in their departments are looked after properly. They may have a special interest in a particular species. Many zoos keep species that are in danger of becoming extinct in the wild. An important part of zoo work is to make sure these animals mate and have babies. Curators are often the people who are specially concerned about these rare animals. They may learn more about a particular species by studying it in the wild, reading about it, and meeting with other experts.

The curators, together with the director, often decide what new animals the zoo needs and take steps to obtain them. This used to be exciting work. Until about fifty years ago, zoos

LEFT: The staff at Britain's Jersey Wildlife Trust have worked hard to save endangered species such as this ring-tailed lemur.

BELOW: The beautiful Sumatran tiger is one of the most endangered subspecies of tiger. It's quite easy to breed in captivity, but its wild habitat is disappearing rapidly. One day soon, there may be no wild Sumatran tigers, only captives.

sometimes sent expeditions to faraway places to search for animals to bring back to the zoo. William Mann, for example, who was director of the National Zoological Park in Washington, D.C., led a number of animal-collecting expeditions in the 1920s and 1930s. Some of these expeditions lasted more than a year and resulted in the capture of thousands of animals. Imagine how thrilled everyone was when the ship carrying all these animals arrived in the United States!

Obtaining new animals is both less exciting and more difficult nowadays. There are fewer animals in the wild, and there are more laws to protect those that are left. Curators — and keepers, too — often talk to people at other zoos about the animals they would like to have. Their discussions occasionally result in a deal of some kind, in which animals are bought, sold, loaned, or traded. Then curators or keepers may find themselves on their way to another zoo, perhaps in an airplane with a caged bird on the next seat, or in a van that's been loaded down with boxes of bats.

The Great Mongoose Caper

Occasionally, curators may travel to a faraway country, as zoo people did in the old days, to find a rare species of animal.

The Liberian mongoose was unknown to people outside Africa when, in 1957, a scientist visiting Liberia, in western Africa, found three

---

World's Biggest Zoo

The San Diego Wild Animal Park in Escondido, California, occupies 735 ha (1820 acres), making it the biggest zoo that's open to the public in the world.

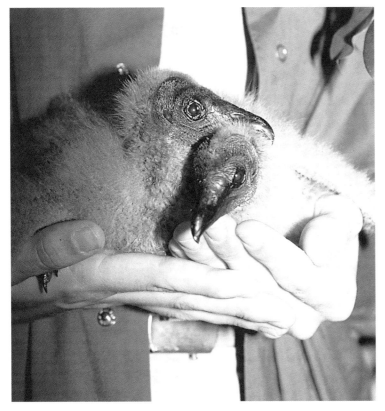

A keeper holds a pair of North African black vultures at Busch Gardens, Florida. Like many other zoos, Busch Gardens works hard to breed animals, especially if they're endangered.

skeletons that were unlike those of any animal he knew. He wrote about his discovery in a scientific journal. Even after the article was published, however, no one in Europe or America knew what the Liberian mongoose looked like. There had never been one in a zoo. There wasn't even a drawing or photograph of one.

Then, a few years ago, the government of Liberia asked the Metro Toronto Zoo and the Royal Ontario Museum to plan an expedition to look for Liberian mongooses and to suggest ways to make sure the species would survive in the wild. The curator of mammals at the zoo was among the group of scientists who accepted the invitation. The group didn't intend to send a mongoose back to Canada. It only meant to find out more about where and how this mongoose lives.

The first expedition was almost a complete failure. The members of the expedition never did see a live Liberian mongoose. The only one they saw had been caught in a trap by people who lived near a forest — and it was dead.

The following year, the same group set out again for Africa. This time it was more fortunate. The curator from the zoo came upon another mongoose that had been trapped and injured, but this one was still alive. The curator bought the animal from the trapper. He examined it and decided that he couldn't set it loose again: it would never have survived because of its injured leg. As a result, the Toronto zoo became the only zoo in the world to have a Liberian mongoose in its collection. (And this may be the only book in the world to have its photograph.)

In the spring of 1993, staff from the zoo and the Royal Ontario Museum again set out for western Africa. They hoped this time to find a mate for the mongoose at the zoo. This trip, like the first one, was disappointing. No live mongoose was discovered. Chances are there are very few remaining, and it may not be possible to save the species. That same year, sadly, the mongoose at the zoo died.

The Metro Toronto Zoo and the Royal Ontario Museum together sent a group of scientists and staff (below) to Africa's west coast to investigate the wildlife there and suggest ways to preserve it. They came back with the first Liberian mongoose (left) to live in any zoo, anywhere.

57

SHOULD ZOO ANIMALS DO TRICKS?

Years ago, an Asian elephant called Paulina helped to build the Detroit Zoo. She pulled carts full of lumber and pushed fallen trees aside. Trucks got stuck in the mud, but Paulina didn't.

John T. Millen, the director of the Detroit Zoo in Michigan, used a megaphone to make sure people heard him when he introduced Paulina to visitors on opening day.

At Hagenbeck's zoo in Germany, many different animals — even polar bears — were trained to do tricks to amuse visitors.

Paulina wasn't just a pretty face; she was a worker. And after the zoo opened, she kept on working. She gave rides to thousands of visitors. For many of them, Paulina was the best part of the zoo.

Not only elephants but also a number of other animals have been trained to give rides or entertain visitors at the zoo. For many years, keepers taught chimpanzees

because someone has made them do it.

People who work with animals in the zoo have a different point of view. Almost everyone agrees that the Chimpanzees' Tea Party was a dumb idea. The chimpanzees looked silly and people laughed at them. That's wrong. But elephants and several other zoo animals seem to like doing things with their keepers. Because they are not living in the wild, they can easily get bored.

Elephants, apes, and seals all seem healthier, more alert, and more active if an effort is made to do things with them. Not every keeper has the skill to work well with these animals, but some keepers do. Their kind of training is good for the animals and gives visitors a chance to see how clever or strong the animals are.

to eat off plates and drink from cups and saucers. The Chimpanzees' Tea Party was a big hit at the London Zoo until it was stopped in the 1970s.

Some people today think it's wrong to train wild animals to obey any human command. They think it's cruel to make an animal do anything it would not do by itself. They say that elephants give rides and chimpanzees eat off plates only

Thousands of people came every day in the summer months to see the Chimpanzees' Tea Party at the London Zoo. It was stopped in the 1970s.

Animal Doctors

It takes seven or eight years of study to become an animal doctor, or veterinarian. That's as long as it takes to become a doctor who treats human patients. The university degree, however, is just the beginning of a zoo vet's training.

What vets learn at university usually prepares them to treat only domestic animals. They learn about pets, such as dogs and cats, parrots and canaries, and farm animals, such as horses and cows, pigs and sheep. Very few veterinary students get the chance to treat a reticulated python, ring-tailed lemur, or rhinoceros. So when young vets report for work at the zoo for the first time, they may run into some tricky problems.

Household pets and farm animals are used to being around all kinds of people. Zoo animals are not. Fairly small zoo animals may panic when a person who is not their keeper comes too close to them. They may squirm or bite when a new vet touches them. They may try to escape if not tightly held. Large animals, such as bison, big cats, apes, and elephants, may attack a strange person who comes too close to them. Such attacks can be disastrous.

Tom Dunstan, who was a keeper many years ago at a small zoo in southern Ontario, remembered that he used to be sent into the cage with any animal that had to be examined. If it was a big and dangerous animal, Tom went

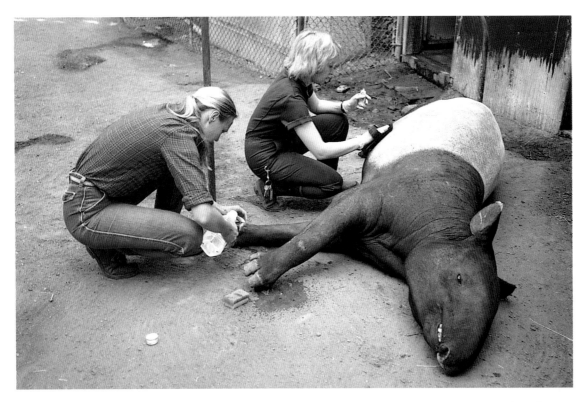

ABOVE: A zoo veterinarian examines a Malayan tapir that has been given a tranquilizer.

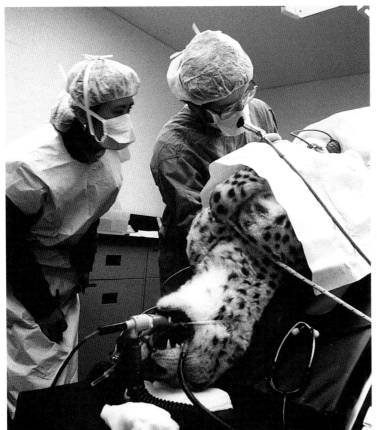

LEFT: These vets are examining a cheetah to find out if it can become a mother — part of the zoo's work to preserve an endangered species.

61

WHAT HAPPENS WHEN ZOO ANIMALS DIE?

Many animals actually live longer in the zoo than they would in the wild. Animals that might be attacked and eaten by predators in natural conditions are safe in the zoo. There is never a drought or famine in the zoo, as there sometimes is in the wild; zoo animals always have water and food. Old and weak animals that might perish in the wild are cared for in the zoo. And vets in the zoo treat wounds and diseases that in the wild might be fatal.

Still, thousands of animals die in zoos each year. They die as a result of accident, disease, or old age. Most zoos have an arrangement with a private firm to dispose of the dead animals. Usually they're cremated.

Some zoos have specially trained vets, called veterinary pathologists, who examine the bodies of dead animals before they are taken away. The pathologist may discover, for example, that an animal was not getting enough of a certain mineral or vitamin in its food. Or he or she may find that the animal was suffering from an ailment the keepers hadn't noticed.

This information is useful to the keepers who work with the animals every day. They can add minerals or vitamins to the animals' diet. If they know that a species tends to develop a certain disease, they can watch for symptoms and perhaps treat a sick animal in time to prevent its death.

Sometimes, veterinarians learn more about an animal when it is dead than when it was alive. And when an animal dies, it sometimes provides information that prolongs the lives of others of its kind.

in with a rope tied into a big loop at the end of a pole. His job was to flip the rope over the animal's neck, tighten it, and hold the animal steady while the vet checked it out. In most zoos now, neither keepers nor vets are allowed to go into cages with dangerous animals. Instead, the animal may be held in a special small cage while the vet examines it through the bars. Or it may be given a drug to make it sleep for a while.

Vets use special devices to shoot a hypodermic needle into the animal to make it sleep. The needle contains a drug that is released as soon as it hits. It sounds easy, but it isn't. For one thing, zoo animals often get to know what the device — and the vet — looks like. As soon as they see either of them, they do their best to make themselves become a difficult target. For another thing, the vet can often only estimate how much drug is needed. To get the amount exactly right, so that the animal is down only as long as necessary and no more, it is necessary to know how much the animal weighs and when it last ate. Often the vet has to guess.

Vets, like everyone else at the zoo, are learning more about wild animals all the time. They learn from one another. Sometimes they travel to countries where the animals live naturally and study them in their wild habitat. A number of zoos and other organizations work hard to share what they have learned. They hold conferences and workshops and publish journals. By going to the meetings and reading the articles, zoo people continue to get better at what they do. With this knowledge, a little luck, and a lot of love, they help animals in the zoo to live longer and more contented lives than ever before.

DISAPPEARING ANIMALS

Visitors to Africa two hundred years ago were amazed by what they saw. One hunter and explorer described the continent as a "fairyland of sport" because there were so many animals, and they were all so tame. Among the many species he saw was the springbok, a beautiful antelope with a red coat and black and white markings. Tens of thousands of springbok would gather in the valleys in the spring. The noise their hooves made when they struck the ground was like the sound of drums and could be heard far away. Today people hardly ever see more than a couple of dozen springbok at one time.

Animals were plentiful in North America, too. Bison, for example, gathered on the western plains in herds of a hundred thousand or more. In Europe, when certain species of geese migrated, they covered the sky. Some species still exist in such abundance, but not many. The time has passed when the numbers of animals in the world made humans seem negligible.

OPPOSITE PAGE: Gerald Durrell, famous all over the world for the books he has written about animals, started a zoo in Jersey called the Jersey Wildlife Trust. This zoo was among the first to make natural-seeming exhibits for many animals, including gorillas.

Zoos have sometimes been the last home of animals that have become extinct. The last known quagga (right) died in the Amsterdam Zoo in Holland, while the last Tasmanian wolf, or thylacine (below), died in the Hobart Zoo in Australia.

Because there were so many animals in those days, hardly anyone worried very much if the ones in the zoo died. They could always send hunters to get more from the wilderness. Many years passed before people understood that if they kept taking animals out of the wilderness, one day there would be no animals — and no wilderness — left.

The quagga was a kind of zebra with stripes on only the front half of its body. Once there were so many quaggas in southern Africa that it

An animal is said to be extinct when no one has seen it alive in the wild over a period of 50 years. It has been longer than that since anyone saw a Syrian wild ass.

never occurred to anybody to worry about them. Settlers killed them and used their skins to make water bottles. People were still using water bottles made of quagga skin in the late nineteenth century. But by then there were no more quaggas. The last known quagga died in the Amsterdam Zoo in 1883.

Sadly, zoos have been the last home of several animals that have become extinct, which means that they no longer exist anywhere on earth. Thylacines, also called Tasmanian wolves, were lean and fierce-looking animals. The last known thylacine died in an Australian zoo in the early 1900s. About a hundred years ago, there were millions of passenger pigeons in North America. People ate them. They were so easy to catch that hunters simply hung nets from trees and caught pigeons in the air like fish in the sea. In fact, they were too easy to catch. The last known passenger pigeon died in the Cincinnati Zoo in 1914.

When the world was full of all kinds of animals, zoos existed mainly to show people what they were like. Now that many animals are in danger of becoming extinct, zoos are trying to keep endangered species alive. No zoo wants to be the owner of the last animal of its kind.

Hard Choices

Zoo directors and the people who work with them have some hard decisions to make. They can't save all the endangered species. Zoos aren't big enough, for one thing. If all the zoos in the world were put together, they would cover an area about the size of Brooklyn, which is just a fraction of New York City. That is not nearly enough space to shelter all the endangered animals. For another thing, zoo people don't know enough about all the endangered animals to be able to save them. They are learning more all the time, but time is running out. They can't afford to make mistakes. Finally, zoos have only so much money. They have to think carefully about how that money is spent.

A zoo in a northern climate, where the winters are long and cold, has to spend a lot of money to keep animals from tropical regions alive. Zoos in Toronto, Chicago, and New York, for example, all have beautiful pavilions to hold animals from southern countries. Some of these pavilions are like huge greenhouses. They are filled with plants — vines, ferns, and tropical trees — and animals, such as toucans, jaguars, and capybaras, that live naturally in rainforests and might not survive the winter if they were kept outside.

Such buildings are wonderful. There is something magical about walking through a glass-covered rainforest when there is snow on the ground outside. Visitors see animals they might never see if the zoo didn't keep them. But these buildings are expensive to heat and maintain. In some ways, it would make more sense for northern zoos to spend their money on animals that can live with cold weather and deep snow.

The Salmonier Nature Park in Newfoundland, Canada — where the winters are very hard — keeps only animals that live naturally in that part of the world. They raise the Arctic hare, which used to be common in Newfoundland and Labrador, but is now scarce. Similarly, the Edinburgh Zoo in Scotland has built a special park for animals that were plentiful in that country long ago. They have wolves, bears, lynx, wild boar, red grouse, and deer, all of which roam in outdoor pens. The Minnesota Zoo in the United States also has set aside a part of its grounds for animals, such as beaver and pronghorn antelope, that might have lived in the state before the cities were built.

Most zoos keep some animals that are expensive to feed and maintain mainly because visitors expect to see them. Koalas, for example, eat only the young leaves from eucalyptus trees. People can grow eucalyptus in San Diego, California, which is good news for the koalas at the San Diego Zoo. But eucalyptus is not easy to grow in Philadelphia, Pennsylvania. Consequently, eucalyptus leaves for the koalas at the Philadelphia Zoo must be flown in every week from the west coast of the United States.

It costs a lot of money to feed an elephant, too. For the same amount of money, the zoo could keep a bunch of chimpanzees or a small herd of antelope. But if there were no elephants, some people might decide not to visit the zoo. And if fewer paying customers visit the zoo, then it will have less money to spend on the animals.

Zoo directors, helped by the people who work with them, have to decide what the zoo can do to save endangered animals and, at the same time, make sure visitors keep on coming.

Keeping in Touch

The Frankfurt Zoo in Germany was badly damaged by bombs during the Second World War. By the time the war ended in 1945, parts of the zoo had been reduced to rubble. Dr. Bernhard Grzimek was the director in charge of rebuilding it. He made it one of the world's great zoos, with spectacular and beautiful exhibits that featured many unusual species. Dr. Grzimek was also a scientist and author. He wrote an animal encyclopedia and a number of entertaining memoirs about his life with animals.

In his books Dr. Grzimek described the work he did to help protect wild animals in their native countries. He was especially concerned about the survival of wildlife in western Africa. Dr. Grzimek knew there would be no zoos if there were no wild places to provide them with animals. He made sure the Frankfurt Zoo gave money to people who worked in Africa to preserve the wilderness.

Germany's Frankfurt Zoo gave Mark and Delia Owens this truck to help them get around Botswana's rugged landscape.

The Frankfurt Zoo still supports the work of scientists and conservationists in Africa. It has given money, for example, to two American scientists, Mark and Delia Owens, who started important conservation projects in Botswana and Zambia. Other zoos support similar projects in other parts of the world.

An organization called Wildlife Conservation International (WCI) is connected to the Bronx Zoo in New York. WCI has given money to scientists and conservationists all over the world. It has helped set up protected parks for jaguars in central America. It has helped set up programs to save the black rhinoceros. Like other species of rhinoceros, the black rhino is endangered because some people believe its horn, when ground up into a powder, has magical powers. Poachers killing the black rhino for its horn have destroyed all but a couple of thousand of them. WCI has also provided money to scientists counting elephants in Africa. Counting animals is one of the first things scientists do in order to conserve them. They have to know how many animals there are before they can decide if they are in danger.

Besides contributing to conservation projects overseas, most zoos keep one, two, or several special animals. They may have a pair of mountain gorillas, of which there are only a few hundred in the world. Or they may have a pair of Rothschild's mynahs (a beautiful bird from an island off the coast of Africa), or a pair of Sumatran tigers, which are also rare. Usually,

The Owenses, shown here in the house they built in North Luangua National Park, Botswana.

73

WHERE DO ZOO ANIMALS COME FROM?

The first zoo animals were often gifts from people who kept wild animals as pets. A gorilla called Massa, for example, who lived at the Philadelphia Zoo for many years, was the gift of a woman who had a passion for apes. Massa had been raised to wear dresses, so no one should have been surprised that he thought he was a female human. He was introduced to female gorillas, but he refused to have anything to do with them. He preferred people until the day he died.

For a long time, zoos got most of

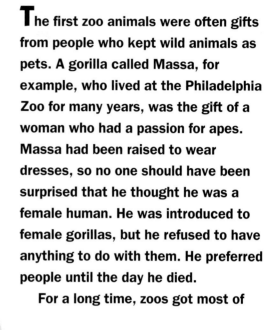

When an animal trainer, Gertrude Lintz, found the lowland gorilla, Massa, in the 1930s, it was sick and seemed to be dying. She nursed it back to health and eventually gave it to the Philadelphia Zoo in Pennsylvania. Massa lived at the zoo until he died in 1984.

when a zoo is working to preserve endangered animals like these, the keepers and curators keep in touch with scientists working in the animals' natural homes. Occasionally, they even send zoo-raised animals back to their home range, to try to preserve the species in the wild.

their stock from dealers who bought and sold wild animals. The earliest dealers set up shop near the docks in major ports. There they would do business with the captains and officers of sailing ships that made voyages around the world. And there the zoo directors, and people who wanted wild animals for their private collections, would come to buy them.

Some twentieth-century dealers did more than just buy and sell animals. Men like Carl Hagenbeck of Hamburg, Germany, and Frederik Zeehandelaar of New Jersey took orders for particular animals and planned expeditions to capture them. Some of the people who captured animals became famous. An American hunter, Frank Buck, wrote a book about his adventures called *Bring 'Em Back Alive*, which millions of young people read in the 1950s.

Today, many wild animals are becoming endangered, and laws have been passed in many countries to stop people from capturing them. Smugglers still capture some animals illegally for sale to private collectors. But most zoos obey the laws meant to protect animals. They encourage animals in their collections to mate, so that their babies will replace the animals that grow old and die in the zoos. Many zoos also get some of the animals they need from other zoos. The animals may be traded, borrowed, or bought.

The cost of a zoo animal can vary a lot. Because some species breed easily in captivity but are quite hard to take care of, zoos almost give them away. Big cats such as lions and jaguars are cheap and fairly easy to get if a zoo has the staff and space to keep them. But a well-behaved female elephant that has been trained to respond to its keeper's commands may cost around $80 000.

The Case of the Arabian Oryx

The Arabian oryx is a species of antelope with a creamy-white hide and long, slender horns. Seen sideways it looks like a unicorn.

Until about fifty or sixty years ago, many Arabian oryx lived in the desert regions of the

Arabian oryx have been released into a number of protected parks in the Middle East, including this one in Hai-Bar, Israel.

Arabian peninsula. They ate grass and desert plants and sometimes had to travel great distances to find water. They were very tough animals. They had to be: they lived in a region that has little water or vegetation. But they were not tough enough to withstand bullets.

About forty years ago, scientists realized the Arabian oryx was almost extinct. People had moved into the lands where it lived, and some of them were hunting it for its meat, hide, and horns. In 1960, there may have been no more than thirty Arabian oryx left in the world.

Usually, the best way to protect an endangered animal is to make sure that it is left undisturbed in its natural home. But there was no way to stop the hunting completely. And the remaining Arabian oryx were so few and scattered so widely that it was unlikely the population would recover without human help. It was a situation that called for fast, drastic action.

In 1962, an expedition was sent into the desert to save the few Arabian oryx that were left. Several conservation organizations provided money and supplies. Great Britain's Royal Air Force helped out by lending an airplane. A company that provided guides and equipment for African safaris gave tents and trucks.

It was no easy matter to find a wild Arabian oryx. It was even harder to catch one. The conservationists in their trucks followed the animals across the stony ground. When they got close they tried to lasso them, but they had to be very careful not to hurt them. The expedition managed to capture three Arabian oryx: two males and one female. The three were sent first to Kenya and then to the zoo in Phoenix, Arizona, which had been chosen as its last refuge. The desert in Arizona is a lot like the animal's Arabian home.

Happily, a few more oryx were found to keep the threesome company. The London Zoological Society gave its Arabian oryx to the Phoenix Zoo. Then the rulers of Saudi Arabia and Kuwait added the handful of oryx from their private zoos. And soon, one of the female oryx at Phoenix gave birth to a baby. So by about 1970, it appeared there might still be a chance to save the species.

The keepers at the Phoenix Zoo endured many sleepless nights worrying about their rare antelopes. At first, they didn't know what to feed them. They tried a number of different kinds of hay and manufactured pellets before they were satisfied with the result. There was always a chance that some disease would kill all the oryx in a few days. Antelopes can get the same diseases that other hoofed animals, such as horses and cattle, sometimes get. An outbreak of hoof-and-mouth disease or tuberculosis would have put a quick end to the rescue effort.

Luckily, the herd in Phoenix survived the first few years. More female oryx gave birth to baby oryx, which grew up strong and healthy. By the late 1970s, Phoenix was able to send oryx to zoos in San Diego, Los Angeles, and Texas.

Best of all, ten years later the American zoos sent some Arabian oryx back to their original homes. Protected parks were set up in Saudi Arabia, Jordan, and Israel. Here the oryx were turned loose to live as they had once lived in the wild. But now they were protected: the parks were fenced and guarded by rangers. An animal that had been nearly wiped off the face of the earth got a chance to start again. There should still be Arabian oryx a hundred years from now.

Tiger Poo?

A number of zoos sell the dung the keepers take out of the animal enclosures to the public for use in their gardens.

78

What Zoos Can Do

A deer native to China, called Père David's deer, was already extinct in the wild when people in the west first learned about it in the 1860s. All the surviving animals were kept in the Imperial Hunting Park outside Beijing. An English aristocrat, the eleventh Duke of Bedford, had a passion for exotic animals. Somehow he managed to obtain a few for his private zoo. It was fortunate that he did because a few years later there was a war in China in which the Père David's deer all perished. The Duke of Bedford's herd was all that remained of this unusual species. Today, there are herds of Père David's deer in zoos and parks all over the world.

A few species exist in the world today because they have found homes in zoos. Przewalski's wild horse was kept alive in zoos after it had ceased to exist in its natural habitat in central Asia.

79

ABOVE: **The highly endangered golden-lion tamarin has been at the center of a remarkable zoo program. A number of animals have been successfully released into a protected park in Brazil thanks mainly to the National Zoological Park.**

RIGHT: **Two Andean condors at the zoo in Barquisemeto, Venezuela. Staff at the zoo have cooperated with the San Diego and Los Angeles zoos to raise the birds in captivity, then set them free in the wild. The North American zoos have used what they learned in Venezuela to help them in their work with the even rarer California condor.**

Zoos have saved other species as well. Przewalski's wild horse, the wisent, the California condor, and the Nene goose have all been kept alive in zoos when they were extinct, or nearly extinct, in the wild.

Many other species continue to survive in the wild but are becoming rare. A pretty and nimble little monkey-like creature called the golden-lion tamarin, for example, lives in a tiny bit of rainforest on the coast of Brazil. Its forest habitat was once much larger than it is today, but people have cut down the trees. A number of zoos, led by the National Zoological Park in Washington, have kept groups of these animals alive in captivity. Some golden-lion tamarins that were raised in zoos have been sent back to Brazil, just as the oryx were returned to the Middle East.

It would be encouraging to think that

80

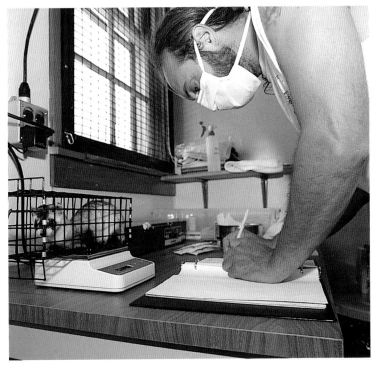

ABOVE: This black-bellied pangolin (also called a scaly anteater) is not on display at the Metro Toronto Zoo. Staff members are doing special research in the back rooms of the zoo to discover what it eats and how best to keep it.

LEFT: The black-footed ferret was on the edge of extinction when zoos set out to try to rescue them. This ferret is in a restraining cage both for its own and the keeper's safety while it is being weighed.

Play Ball!

Zookeepers are always trying to find stuff for the animals to play with. They give lions and tigers "tiger balls," for example. These are big — about 60 cm (2 feet) high — hard, plastic balls that the animals can climb on or bat around. The trouble with all such toys, however, is that the animals may break them or throw them at visitors. Elephants and orangutans can break just about anything. And chimpanzees throw small objects as hard and accurately as big-league baseball players.

zoo-raised animals could always be returned to the wild. But it is never an easy thing to do. The Arabian oryx, for example, were accustomed to being fed by humans. It took a long time to get them used to the idea that they had to fend for themselves.

The zoo-raised tamarins had an even harder time learning how to survive in the rainforest. The first ones sent back to Brazil weren't used to climbing on branches that jiggled and bounced — in the zoo, they had been given only rigid poles and bars to play on. They hadn't a clue how to find food. Scientists and their helpers hoisted the boxes the tame tamarins lived in high into the tops of trees in the rainforest. They kept feeding them until, over time, the animals started to make little trips in the treetops themselves to explore and browse and find fresh fruit. After a while, some of the tame tamarins met wild ones. The wild ones taught them what they needed to know to survive. But not all the tame animals got along with the wild ones. A lot of them died before they learned what they needed to know in order to live in the wild.

Zoos can't hope to save all the species that are endangered, but they *can* do a number of useful things. People working in zoos can study different animals to help discover what they need in order to survive. Zoos themselves can be used to demonstrate what wild animals are like. They can show animals that people seem instinctively to like: the graceful big cats, powerful bears, and sleek wolves. Zoos can also display the animals that humans sometimes dislike or find hard to understand: armadillos and aardvarks, eels and vultures, stick insects and bats. Zoos can help people see how different all these animals are and how marvelous each one is in its own way, so they will want to do something to save the wilderness where the wild animals live. Finally, zoos can give money, supplies, and expert assistance to scientists and conservationists who are working to protect the wilderness. That way, every visitor to the zoo not only learns about wild animals but also helps keep them alive each time a ticket is bought at the zoo's front gate.

FUTURE ZOOS

You are walking along a winding path through a green, leafy forest. You hear the chirping and twittering of birds all around you. From somewhere ahead you can make out the sound of rushing water. It gets louder as you make your way along the path. You must be getting closer to the place where the sound is coming from. Presently, you arrive at a clearing. You pause for a moment. After your long walk in the shade of tall trees, the bright sunlight dazzles you. You stop to catch your breath and let your eyes get used to the brightness.

Then you see the grizzly bear.

It seems to be no more than a meter or two away. There is no fence between it and you. There is nothing at all, as far as you can see, to stop the bear from joining you on the path. For a moment you forget where you are. You're scared.

But the grizzly takes no notice of you. It is standing at the edge of a fast-moving river,

OPPOSITE PAGE: Butterflies, like this gray pansy butterfly, have the freedom of the Malayan Woods Pavilion at the Metro Toronto Zoo.

85

WHAT'S A ZOO DO?

gazing into the water. It is perfectly still. The sunlight is reflected on the glossy black and white hairs on its back. A fine spray of water has made its muzzle wet. The bear's eyes are shining. When it moves, it moves so swiftly that you don't really see what has happened. Only afterward do you realize it must have moved, because what you see now is different from what you saw before. In that instant the grizzly plucked a fish out of the water. Now it cradles the fish in its paws and begins to eat.

The Perfect Zoo

Jon Coe, an architect based in Philadelphia, draws plans for new zoo exhibits. He made up the story about the grizzly bear to show what he thinks a trip to the zoo should be like. Visitors should be able to forget they are in a zoo, he says. They should imagine, for a while, that they are in the wilderness. When they see an animal, they should first see what it looks like. But they should also see how it behaves in its proper habitat. They should see how fast it can move and how it eats. They should understand that it doesn't need people to get by.

In the zoo Jon Coe likes to imagine, animals act just as if they were living in a wild place. They sleep, explore, find food, and deal with other animals, exactly as if they were in their natural home.

This zoo may be a long way off. Many zoos

have got rid of the cages and walls that made old zoos look like prisons. And a number of zoos have created exhibits where visitors can easily pretend that they are seeing animals in the wild. The hard part in making the perfect zoo is building an exhibit in which animals can behave as if they really were wild.

This is because zookeepers need to control the animals in a lot of important ways. They decide when and what the animals eat, where they spend their days, and what other animals they mix with. They determine what the exhibit is made of. Often, what you see in the exhibit isn't even real: the rocks may be made of concrete, the trees may be wrapped in fiberglass bark, and the vegetation may be either fake or planted out of the animals' reach. Zookeepers don't create these conditions because they want the animals to be deprived of things they need. They do it so they can keep the animals clean, healthy, safe, and properly fed.

In the perfect zoo, the animals would have to accept the fact that people were around and watching them, because that's part of what a zoo does. But they would also practice behaviors exactly like those that come to them naturally in the wild. They would hunt or forage for food; sense danger and hide; experience storms and droughts; come into contact with real trees, bushes, rivers, and streams.

The staff at the National Zoological Park in Washington, D.C., has made a special effort to keep animals you don't often see in zoos. This keeper is giving visitors a close-up look at a horseshoe crab.

For now, while many zoo exhibits may look like real wilderness to visitors, they may only be more-or-less comfortable enclosures from the animals' point of view. Perhaps, one day, zoo designers will find a way to put it all together, to fix it so that visitors can watch in breathless silence while a grizzly bear fishes in a river under a blazing afternoon sun. Meanwhile, zoos will go on doing what they do now, which is to remind us how important wild places and the animals that inhabit them really are.

Acknowledgments

Thanks to Toby Styles, Tom Mantil, Francis Faigal, and other members of the staff of the Metro Toronto Zoo who commented on early versions of the manuscript and supplied illustrative material. Brian Beck gave advice and time and expended considerable effort to supply suitable photographs. Peter de Groot of the Royal Ontario Museum described the expeditions to Liberia and the Ivory Coast. Chuck Doyle at Burnet Park Zoo in Syracuse, New York, told me all about Tundi and supplied photographs. John Edwards, zoo historian, opened up his archive of zoo postcards and was generous in sharing zoo lore. I am indebted to many people from zoos across North America, and especially to members of the Elephant Managers Association, who have allowed me to audit their conferences and consented to be interviewed.

Index

WHAT'S A ZOO DO?